Books by Vicki Rickabaugh

Gateway to the Universe:
Knowing Your Inner Self, 2010

Spirits United:
The Sacred Connection, 2010

Spirits United
The Sacred Connection

Vicki Rickabaugh

Photographs by Pamela Turner

Published by Interwoven Connections
Howell, NJ, USA

The author gratefully acknowledges the contributions of additional photographs, used with permission.

Photographs on page 22, 80, 104, and 116, courtesy of Cara and Tom Tozour, Fidler Run Farm.

Photographs on page 20, 54, and 72, courtesy of Paula and David Sagui.

Photographs on page 40 and 78, courtesy of Dr. Iris Biely.

Published by
Interwoven Connections
PO Box 686
Howell, NJ 07731
www.interwovenconnectionspubs.com

ISBN-13: 978-0-9829582-1-6

Dedication

For my Guardian Angel who has given me belief,
inner tranquility, stillness and strength.

Even though I will only know your spirit for the moment,
the merging of the spirits will be forever.

Fatima, I dedicate this book to you,
the extraordinary being who has shown me
the glowing light within today and tomorrow.
This is the beauty of the moment with all its grace and glory.

Acknowledgements

With my husband Rick, love allows our hearts to embrace
all the seasons of life with joy, happiness, and trust.
To see and feel the colors of the universe
is truly love; it is an awakening.

My children and grandchildren–Gloria, George, Peggy, Marc,
Jenny, Kirsten, Ashley, Michael, Nicole and Mya–
You will walk down many paths in your lives.
Wherever the journey takes you,
know that you will always be loved.
Your spirit is within me
and my spirit will always be a part of you.

I honor my mother, Marilyn:
the depth of my gratitude is like the universe,
it is immeasurable.

For Pam, my spirit sister,
In the reflection of you, I have seen myself,
and that has changed my life forever.

With all the kindness and compassion that embraces who you are, Iris, thank you for the journey.

To Bubbles and Joe: The giving or receiving of a gift cannot compare to the knowing of the true gift itself. You are gentle souls who softly touch many.

I could not have found my way and continued on this path alone. I would like to thank those who have walked along with me, giving of themselves and adding their uniquely individual colors to my life:
Lee and Warren, Margaret, Syd,
Ellie FGM and Hugh, Nicole and Joel, Leslie and Dan,
Shell and Sharon, Linda and Nelson, Judy
Nancy, Larry, Steven, JoAnne, Katherine,
Karl, Barbara and Joe, Linnea, Kem, Joyce
Sara, Gina, Ken, Liz and Chrissy,
Stephanie, Jessica, Christin, Paula and David,
Hannelore, Sherry, Alyson, and Mary.

THE HORSE

Majestic,
gentle,
A trusting partner.

He is of strength and power,
yet there is a stillness that resides within.

He desires only love,
compassion and understanding,
and in return
he will be your sacred friend.

It is not a coincidence that energy and spirit
meet, sharing and giving of one another.

It is pure consciousness.

There is a reason and a purpose,
created by life's forces and omnipresent
energies that present themselves to each other.

The sharing and giving
becomes an irreplaceable gift.

I whisper in your ear and you hear my
dreams and aspirations.

You sing to my heart whenever we are near.

I sing back in refrain, our voices becoming one.

My spirit will always dance with your spirit.
Our spirits will always dance together.

Once connected, we can never be apart.

Sometimes while walking through life,
the sky gets dark, clouds form, and
an unavoidable storm will be upon you.

Any storm becomes a challenge
for how one will conquer the seemingly
unbearable burdens of
yesterday, today, and tomorrow.

There is no life without storms,
no storm without the emotions that
can shake the very belief of our inner soul,
if we allow it.

Believe,
This is the moment,
and in this moment is the new lighted path.

Behold the universe,
the beauty that resides in all of us!

A happy heart greets the new morn
and sees that all things are possible.

Believe that the universal spirit is seen
and known by you and what you give.

Just think,

Change the core belief

and all things are possible.

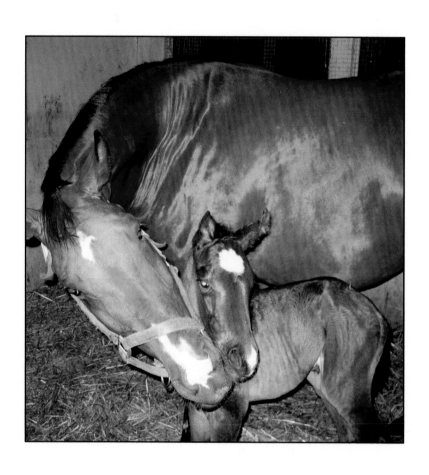

Gently
    Lovingly
        Seeing
            Giving

Sharing
    Knowing
        Believing
            Being
                One

I know that I am different from many,
but I am also the same to a few.

That sameness creates a surge,
an energy in my life
like no other life experience,
so that I may become.

To find the answers of the universe, I must
know and realize the wonder of myself.

When I look within and then express my
thoughts outwardly, I have first gone
beyond the trees and the stars
and into the universe.

There is where I will find all treasures.
If perchance I do not find me out there,
then the universe is not.

But no worry.

I know and see what I have been
searching for is in the now.

That is how we evolve.
This is the moment.

The ultimate gift is the simultaneously
and unconditionally mirrored
giving and receiving,
totally without thought,
with all your heart and soul,
from one being to another.

By giving the gift, in that moment
we become one, connected with a bond
so strong that it cannot be broken.

When a person receives the gift,
one can feel love, happiness, joy,
peace and tranquility.

This is the gift, it is the knowing.

There are many paths,
many journeys,
vast,
beyond the infinite.

This is where
stillness and peace reside,
and where
the soul of the universe
can be seen.

It is the beginning,
where one awakens.

It is the dawn,
the spirit and light
that greets each new day.

Embrace it.
You are the light and spirit
that awakens this day.

Sometimes I wonder
how many times have I met you
on my journey?

I wonder what we were like,
and then I smile.

It does not matter.

I know what we are today,
and I am blessed.

As we live we evolve,
looking introspectively,
reflecting on our feelings and thoughts,
asking who we are
and what we want from life.

May your life be filled with
continual knowledge,
insight and wisdom,
strength and compassion.

Did you ever wonder why people greet
the morning differently than the night?
We wake up and say good morning
to the bright sun, the singing birds,
the colorful flowers and trees.
We are amazed by all the animals
and creatures scampering around.

But what happens to the night?
Do we greet the night while listening
to the voices? Do we look at the moon
and say good night in the same way
we say good morning, seeing the soft hues
reflecting from the moon light?
What about the depth and breadth
of the stars, reaching out into the
universe, asking us to join them?
The day-night is one.

Although there are many wonderful
beings in this world,
many do not wish to understand
what they have not personally experienced.

And do not wish to experience
more than they think they understand.

If I see a horse in flight and describe
only that here is a horse,
then I have separated myself
from that beauty of oneness which is
between the flight of the horse
and the universe.

In my thoughts and actions
I would have conveyed
only the horse.

I would have missed the
simplicity and at the same time
the complexity of the bounding flight.

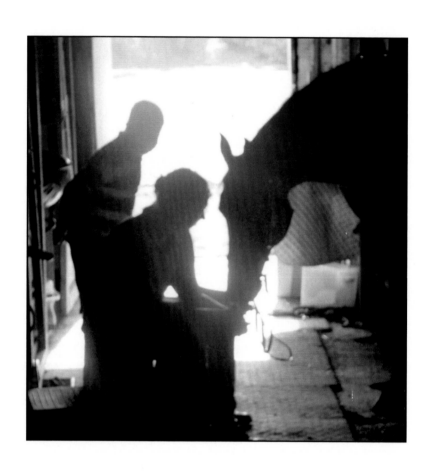

To know silence
is to hear the harmony of all sound.

Peace and stillness
finds its blend.

One sees the unseeable
and knows there is more.

Understand
that every part of ourselves
is and belongs within
that silent space.

Each one of us creates our own boundaries
within the body, mind, and spirit.
We can stay trapped,
imprisoned in these boundaries,
accepting their limitations,
or we can realize that the only limits
in life are the ones we place on ourselves

Soar boundlessly,
knowing the sky is infinite
and so are we.
That is where all life is.
There is where you can find me.

We live in a physical world.

But beyond our physical senses,

beyond this physical realm,

is a portal where visions can be seen

and all is connected.

And when the winds blow so hard

from every direction,

so hard that I cannot stand any longer,

I close my eyes and see your vision,

know your strength

and believe.

I have often been asked

if I ever wonder

whether other people understand

my words or thoughts.

Some will understand less,

but they are no lesser.

And some will understand more,

but they are not greater.

It just is.

To give without expectation,

to love unconditionally,

to share life's sacred spirit with

kindness, understanding, and compassion,

that is our connection,

that is our joy and happiness.

It is only through life's energy

and experiences that one can greet and feel

happiness, love and joy.

Everything else is but an illusion.

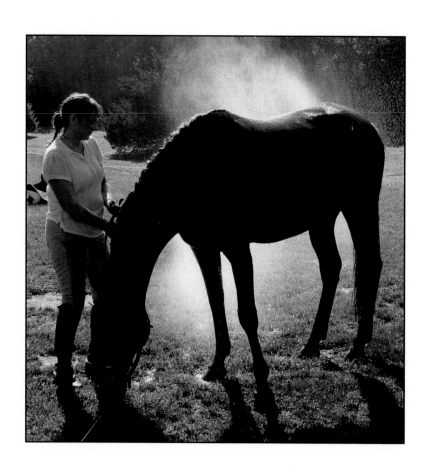

Give for giving's sake,

believe for believing's sake.

Live the moment.

The answers are all within.

I am but a reflection of you
as you are of me,
and all are of the universe.

The body, mind and spirit although one,
grow independently of each other
like the outreaching branches
of a blossoming tree.

Although the branches are separate
they are connected, as they find
their nurturing roots from the earth
and present their gift of life
to the heavens.

The wonders of the world,

the universe, are within.

We are the very existence of all we see.

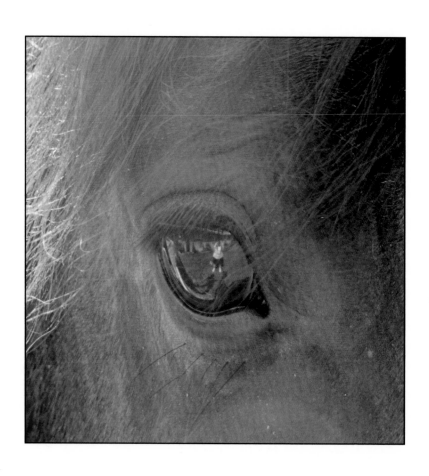

In the reflection of you,

I have seen myself,

and that has changed my life forever.

How beautiful and intricate nature is.

Stop.

Take a moment to see.

Look at the flowers,
the trees,
the birds,
and all living things.

Within,
you can see the universe,
the peace,
the calm.

Life's journey does not "move on"

but instead evolves

while it embraces the past,

the present,

and the future

in the now moment.

Fly with the wind and spirits
to depths unknown.

Know the warmth of the sun
from within all souls.

Dance with the rain drops.

See the reflection of the rainbow
within myself and all.

Every living breathing thing

has a never ending circle of needs.

The circle must stay connected

if we are to exist to our fullest.

We must understand our

complete relationship

with ourselves and

other living things

so that we can obtain

harmony in our daily lives.

Life is a beautiful colored cloth,
and every living breathing thing
is a thread interwoven into this cloth,
to create a wonderful tapestry.

What is life
but to create music
in your heart and soul,
so that the universe
can hear your symphony.

Once you have seen,
you will always know.

Once you know,
the connection will always be.

Greater than words from others
are the words
I hear and sing
within myself.

It started from a distance,
the winds calling to each other,
beckoning to become one.

Sometimes, when I look up into the skies,
I yearn to know what it is that I truly see.

Is this a vision or just the magnificence
within the skies?

Then for a moment, a fleeting moment,
I realize the seeing and knowing is in
the beauty of that moment.

This is what carries one away.

I am where I have never been before
with myself and my relationships.

I trust in you
and put myself in your hands
for safekeeping.

I thank you for all the fulfilling,
gentle yesterdays that you have given me,

and for all the tomorrows that you will bring.

Know that the energy that is within
is part of the whole spirit,
the oneness.

With love and compassion,
this energy will continue to grow
infinitely.

To know the messenger
is to understand the message

The messenger is enveloped within
the message – they are one.

I will always keep open the message
while I hold the messenger deep
within my heart and soul,

For this is where all belief, knowledge,
and truth will be found.

The messenger reveals itself in many
beautiful ways--human forms,
animal spirits, guides and angels.

They all are the creation
from the greatest power.

As messengers
we are reflections of the universe.

Today and every day,
I wish for you to always be embraced
with peace and stillness.
I wish for you the continued vision
to see all of life,
In all its glory,
with the splendor of surrounding colors.

I send to you the warmth and beauty
that radiates from those colors.

May you always be blessed with
spiritual energy.

In life we will travel the path
that some may call our destiny.
Along that path, at times,
we may walk alone or with others.

Sometimes we walk alone because
it may be difficult for the ones we care for,
or those who care for us,
to see or understand
the vision of the path we must take.

Know, as I am sure that you do,
that you will never walk alone.

Your faith, strength, and spirit
are always with you.

And this human spirit,
that believes in all that you are and will be,
will walk the path with you,
in trust and friendship.

The heart is a wonderful and
powerful entity.

It nourishes the body
and reaches out into the ethereal
to connect the spirit and the soul.

But just as our body needs
the heart for nourishment,
so does the spirit and the soul.

Good energy embraces great energy,
and the body, mind, and spirit
will connect, energizing to become
the universal oneness.

The continuation of this amazing force
can only be perpetuated through each other.

The power of one connects
with the power of two.

You are the force

and power

of spiritual energy

that guides and encourages me

along the way.

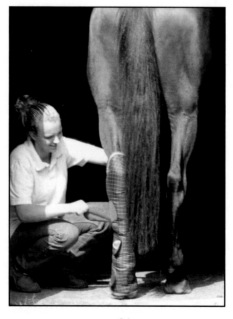

My experiences in life

and awareness of self

and inner truth

will always be a part

of this very special connection.

Gratitude helps one to affirm
and acknowledge the inner self,
the outer self, and beyond.

It gives peace and stillness to the soul
as it opens to the universe.

Because gratitude is a feeling and an
affirmation, there are no limits
to where it can expand.

There are no road blocks,
just an open path to wherever the heart,
soul and unlimited space take you.

I think from the time we are born,
we are taught that life is linear.

Go left right, right left, in out, up down.

Even the ladder of success is thought of
as up down, in a linear direction.

But just think when we were in the womb,
we were in total suspension, floating,
with all of our intended senses,
knowing infinity.

Even though we are in a finite space,
we are part of the infinite universal
vibration, and then we are born.

From that moment most of us spend our lives
just walking, thinking straight.

But there are some of us who will ultimately
find the space-time-beyond continuum.

There we will find a new dimension.

If you focus only
on the journey's end,
you will not be able to clearly see
the path that is in front of you.

The purpose of the body is to house the soul.

That is the meaning of BEING.

To see that which exists without thought,

that is the formless.

This is the infinite spirit

that can coexist with

the form

and the mind.

The ocean –

      mesmerizing,

         strong,

            massive:

As this powerful body of water approaches,
It gently embraces as it greets the shore.
And as I sit and watch, with slow breaths,
I know I am One.

When the day motions to the night
to come forward
and the night becomes quiet and still,
that is when I,
with peace and contentment in my heart,
can find and reflect the moment.
And as the night begins
to merge once again with the day,
that is when I can reach beyond my being
and see the unseeable.
This is where I will meet you.

I have searched for a very long time
for the elusive answers to
life's universal questions.

As I drew closer to some of the answers
and was finally able to hold them
in my grasp, I quickly learned that
universal knowledge cannot be held
in one's grasp.

The hands are not large or strong enough.
Nothing is large enough.

Knowledge is infinite, and shall not be
contained within any boundaries.
What can be contained, is the
quest to obtain the unobtainable.

Daily

May your life be filled with continual
knowledge, insight and wisdom,
strength and compassion.

As we live we evolve, looking
introspectively, reflecting on our
feelings and thoughts, asking who
we are and what we want from this life.

Every motion ripples into another.

Every action creates another action,
which then creates another emotion '
and each is one,
yet interconnected within the circle of life.

Affirmation

We are but reflections of ourselves
and each other.

I am an interconnected, interdependent
spirit, strong yet fragile.

I am where I have never been before
with myself and my relationships.

I trust in you and put myself in
your hands for safekeeping.

I thank you for all the fulfilling, gentle
yesterdays that you have given me,
and for all the tomorrows that you will bring.

When one truly sees another's inner soul,
one sees the universe.

Oneness, illumination,
all that is near creates a heavenly glow,
and the softness of light surrounds.

From the depth of my inner soul
and the extension of my outer soul
I wish for you the greatest energy,
the deepest spiritual fulfillment,
and unbounding love.

For you, the universe should always
open its arms and embrace you.

You are that special.

The glory of prayer is
when one prays the vibration created
echoes softly throughout the universe.

If in this moment of stillness
the words that are uttered
come from a pure heart
with pure intent,
one will be able to feel
the quiet peace.

If every fertile mind
could reap that of which you have planted,
there would be a harvest of kindness and love.
The spirit of peace, happiness, and joy
would fill the universe.

The messenger of light came and gently
touched me with her spirit,
embracing me with kindness,
Compassion, and trust.

The power of love was seen and known.

This is the sacred connection
throughout the universe.

This is the spirit and the message.